WOMAN, NATURE'S HIGHEST ACHIEVEMENT

Mark Severin

EROTIC
BOOKPLATES

AN INTRODUCTION

COLIN R. LATTIMORE

Ex Libris ⁓ L.C.Stolt

SILENT BOOKS
CAMBRIDGE

First published in Great Britain 1990
by Silent Books, Swavesey, Cambridge CB4 5RA

This selection and text © copyright Colin R. Lattimore 1990

Each plate is reproduced with the permission of the present owners.

ISBN 1 85183 022 7

Typeset in Janson (Linotron 202) by Goodfellow & Egan, Cambridge
Printed in Great Britain by Redwood Press Ltd, Melksham, Wiltshire

ACKNOWLEDGEMENTS

I am grateful for the help and support of my fellow committee members of the Bookplate Society in the production of this volume. In particular to James Wilson, Professor William Butler, Maurice Oliver and Benoit Junod for supplying a number of the illustrations and to Professor Butler and our President, Brian North Lee, for help with biographical details.

THE ILLUSTRATIONS

	Artist	*Owner*	*Date*
Front cover	Frank Martin	Benoit Junod	
Endpaper 1	Mark Severin	K. Henderson	1977
Endpaper 2	Mark Severin	E. Young	1958
Frontispiece	Italo Zetti	Gorgio Balbi	1947
Title page	Mark Severin	Lars Stolt	1980
Endpaper 3	Jerzy Drazycki	Michala Kuny	1971
Plate 1	C.W. Sherborn	Robert Day	1894
Plate 2	David Bekker	Boris Levych	1891
Plate 3	Mark Severin	F. Haans	1979
Plate 4	Mark Severin	J. Maeschalek	1982
Plate 5	Mark Severin	R. Hoffsummer	1977
Plate 6	Mark Severin	L. Segers	1973
Plate 7	Mark Severin	S. Golifman	1977
Plate 8	Mark Severin	Mirko Kaizl	1971
Plate 9	Frank Martin	Mark Severin	1956
Plate 10	Eric Gill	Jacob Weiss	1935
Plate 11	Gerard Gaudean	V. Clemmensen	1972
Plate 12	Gerard Gaudean	G. Clemmensen	1972
Plate 13	Gerard Gaudean	J. Vils-Pedersen	1973
Plate 14	Franz von Bayros	G. Wunderlich	1911

THE ILLUSTRATIONS

Why cannot the world understand that morals are simply and purely a matter of taste and cannot be found and extracted from the pages of lawbooks by a couple of old Lesbians and senile eunuchs? Can you find me a pretty young woman or a healthy, strong, virile man whose morals are likely to be affected or endangered by looking at my so-called erotic pictures? I have never discovered such a person. People I know, men and women, have either laughed if the picture was amusing or admired it if it was well executed and tasteful. And five minutes later they neither worried about it nor gave it another thought – because they were sound in body and mind.

'Sur ma morale' (About my morals)
Franz von Bayros, 1866–1924

THERE are still a larger number of people including some booksellers who think that bookplates are illustrations taken from books; and 'erotic' can mean different things to different people. It is necessary therefore to define the subject.

Bookplates – or Ex-Libris as they are otherwise called – are small paper illustrations which are gummed inside the front cover of a book to identify the owner. A number of printing processes are used to produce the plates including copper engraving, steel engraving, lithography and various forms of modern process printing. Bookplates were first used in the fifteenth century and consisted originally of the owner's coat of arms, in whole or in part, together with his name. In those days only armigerous people or companies were likely to own libraries. The pure armorial plate remained popular and almost universally used until the second half of the eighteenth century when pictorial plates were introduced. Composition plates representing the owner's interests appeared in the nineteenth century. Erotic plates have been increasing in popularity since the beginning of this century.

What is meant by erotic? This is likely to be the word, together with the illustration on the front cover, which attracted you to this book in the first place. Is there a difference between erotic, pornographic and obscene? Most people would agree that there is, although it may be harder to define than might at first appear. Just as beauty is said to be in the eye of the beholder so to some extent are eroticism, pornography and obscenity. However, this is not the place for a detailed philosophical discussion on the subject.

Briefly, I would suggest the difference is one of degree and good taste. Most people, today, would find what they regard as erotic drawings acceptable and obscene drawings unacceptable. The dictionary definitions may help to some extent. Erotic is defined as – pertaining to the passion of love, to stimulate sexually, sexual excitement; whereas obscene is abominable, disgusting, filthy, indecent, foul, loathsome – offensive to the senses, taste or refinement. Pornography lies somewhere in between. Originally it was related to activities with prostitutes. The use of such terms as 'soft porn' and 'hard porn' implies some form of continuum which at the one end links up with the erotic and at the other with the obscene.

It is to some extent a matter of generation and conditioning. As sexuality forms an important part of our make-up and activity it seems unreasonable to deny its existence, as was done overtly by the Victorians. In today's more permissive age some would say that the pendulum had swung too far the other way – that there is now too much emphasis on sex and sexuality.

Be that as it may, there is now a more enlightened view of sexual activity, where eroticism is recognised and acknowledged. Erotic bookplates have now become an acceptable form of displaying book ownership – more so on the Continent than in this country.

They first began to appear towards the end of the nineteenth century, and arose out of the drawings of such artists as Franz von Bayros and Aubrey Beardsley, both of whom included bookplates amongst their oeuvre.

C.W. Sherborn *Plate 1*

Nude drawing and painting, to say nothing of sculpture, were acceptable to the Victorian elite, provided they were related to antiquity and classical art. One has only to study the annual exhibitions at the Royal Academy if proof is needed. However, the acceptability seemed only to apply to the upper half of the female form; the lower half was often ill-defined or coveed with diaphanous drapery.

Plate 1 shows a superb copper engraving by C. W. Sherborn (1831–1912) for Robert Day J.P., made in 1894. The erotic element, if such it is, is incidental to the whole design. The semi-clad lady depicting the muse of literature would have been acceptable because of its classical allusion. Very few, if any, serious bookplate collectors would ever think of the great master of nineteenth-cetury armorial copper engraving as producing an erotic bookplate; nevertheless, the bare leg and breast would have been regarded as very erotic by some observers of the period.

A design of the same period but of a much more overt erotic nature is seen in *plate 2*. This is by David Bekker (b.1840) of Odessa for Boris Levych, who was his chief patron. Levych is known to have commissioned well over fifty plates from Bekker. In this one two nude beauties carouse in a vat of wine with an elderly man to musical accompaniment. The plate pays homage to the French author François Villon and may well have been intended for use in a collection of his books.

With the advent of photography in the 1840s another art form became available, originally through daguerreotypes and ambrotypes and later through reproducible photographs on paper, cartes de visite and the ubiquitous postcard. However, as photography dealt with real people it was not specially acceptable to display nude photographs publicly. Many were produced for private circulation.

The bookplate is primarily a personal item, displaying the owner's tastes and interests and used for identifying personal property. To this end the majority of English people who use bookplates at all use only one plate, and very rarely is it of an erotic nature. A few who have a greater interest in the subject may use more than one plate for specialised areas of their

HOMMAGE À FRANÇOÏ WILLON

libraries, but even then the number of different plates is usually limited to half a dozen or so, one of which may be erotic.

On the Continent the picture is very different. There not only do people commission bookplates for personal use but also for exchanging with others in order to build up collections. Some of these plates are used purely for the latter purpose and never see the inside of a book. It has to be said that the artistic quality of these plates can vary enormously. Some Continental collectors may have fifty or more personal plates. For some, erotic bookplates are their speciality. There is sometimes a humorous or punning element in the design, often not very subtle – see *plate 22*, for example. The majority of erotic bookplate artists and designers are to be found on the Continent.

Not only do erotic images vary between individuals, but also between generations. Our Victorian forefathers, it would appear, could be turned wild by the glimpse of a pretty ankle inadvertently revealed. In the Edwardian period more emphasis was given to the female figure as a whole with exaggerated curves; in the 1920s the slim boyish figure was all the rage with rather more revealing dresses. After the Second World War underwear was made to be seen and erotic images were conjured up by stockings, suspender belts and bras. Bikini swimsuits, topless bathing, miniskirts and finally full and explicit nudity bring us up to date.

The illustrations in this book show a wide range of erotic images, none more provocative than those by that master of the erotic bookplate Mark Severin (1906–1987). A native of Belgium, he spent many years in Britain before returning to live near Brussels, where he was Professor at the Institut Supérieur des Beaux Arts at Antwerp. He was a prolific artist, producing nearly five hundred bookplates, many of them engraved on copper, a medium in which he specialised from the 1940s onwards. Over half of his output of bookplates were of an erotic nature, depicting the female form, and occasionally the male, in a variety of poses and situations from the almost virginal to the outright sexually explicit with great skill and delicacy. A number of his plates are shown here.

A nice example of his contrasting styles can be seen in *endpapers 1* and *2*. Ostensibly two female nudes, the differences in line and form are subtle yet effective. On the one hand an innocent bride-like figure entitled 'Woman, Nature's Highest Achievement', the halo suggesting innocence and the diaphanous train a bridal figure, further enhanced by the soft light and the protection of the foliage; on the other a similar female figure, but the use of the diaphanous material this time has an entirely different effect. The tilt of the head, the falling hair, the more luscious body all suggest a more wanton figure, the lack of seclusion being emphasised by the more open landscape and distant mountains.

A similar contrast is seen in two other Severin works shown in *plates 3* and *4*. In the one for F. Haans the model is shown posing with a towel before a starlit window. This, combined with the use of the halo effect again, gives a celestial quality with a carefully poised and groomed presentation. The same model shown at rest in the plate for Johnny Maeschalek produces a dishevelled appearance, the ungainly position of the legs giving an effect of anatomical disproportion and inelegance emphasising the contrast between 'on' and 'off' duty.

Severin's skill in depicting the female form in different poses is demonstrated in *plate 5*, for R. Hoffsummer [see also plate 34]. This is one of a number of such multiple-pose plates. It is entitled 'Retreat of Nymphs in the Forest' and shows nine young ladies in relaxed intimacy in the privacy of the wood.

Returning indoors we have the somewhat contrived design for L. Segers shown in *plate 6* and entitled 'Nude With Two Mirrors'. The placing of the mirrors so as to show the interesting parts of the lady's anatomy from a number of angles is quite clever, but the erotic effect probably comes as much from the use of stockings and petticoat as from the nudity itself.

For some men the thought of their partner initiating or taking the active part in lovemaking is particularly stimulating. Such activities are conjured up in two more Severin plates, the title-page plate for Lars Stolt and *plate 7*, for S. Golifman. Both are stereotyped fantasy images. In the first case the eye is drawn directly to the activity itself; in the second it is the facial expression and body position which commands initial attention.

Plate 8, for Mirko Kaizl, shows a scantily clad young lady lying on the grass in what can only be described as an attitude of

Mark Severin   *Plate 3*

Mark Severin *Plate 4*

Mark Severin *Plate 5*

EX LIBRIS
L.SEGERS

Mark Severin *Plate 6*

Mark Severin *Plate 7*

Mark Severin
Plate 8

MS

Frank Martin   *Plate 9*

blatant exhibitionism. The anatomical details and proportions are beautifully delineated and are typical of the majority of Severin's work. That he worked from life can be easily seen. The same model can be recognised in a number of drawings.

As well as being a prolific designer of bookplates Severin was also a collector and had over fifty personal plates for himself and his wife Nina, either commissioned by, or gifted to him. Many of these were an erotic nature, and a particularly fine one is shown in *plate 9*. This is a rare copper engraving by the English bookplate designer and freelance artist, Frank Martin (b.1921). His designs are usually produced as wood engravings. The grace of form is emphasised by the ballet dancer, though she is somewhat better endowed than the majority of ballet dancers.

Another delightful Frank Martin plate is shown on the front cover. Produced for my Bookplate Society colleague Benoit Junod, it shows two nudes of contrasting proportions: one with a blonde ponytail and boyish figure: the other brunette and of a more rounded form.

English bookplate designers are not yet renowned for their erotic plates, but a few have produced some fine designs such as *plate 10*, designed by Eric Gill (1882–1940) in 1935 for Jacob Weiss. The theme of Eve tempted by the serpent is a popular one, handled on this occasion with great charm.

Gill had an influence on Severin's early work and in his turn Severin influenced many developing young artists, including Gerard Gaudean, a fellow Belgian born at St. Nicholas in 1927. Gaudean studied under Severin at the Institut Supérieur des Beaux Arts at Antwerp and later succeeded to his professorial chair there. He has produced over 400 bookplates as wood engravings and a small number on copper. The nude female form features in many of these, often in association with books. Three of his wood engravings appear in *plates 11, 12* and *13*, two for Vagn and Gudrun Clemmensen and one for Jorgen Vils-Pedersen, some of whose other plates feature elsewhere in this volume. This last implies the owner's taste for wine, women and in this case books.

The Croatian artist Franz von Bayros (1866–1924) played an important part in revitalising the art of book illustration. He was

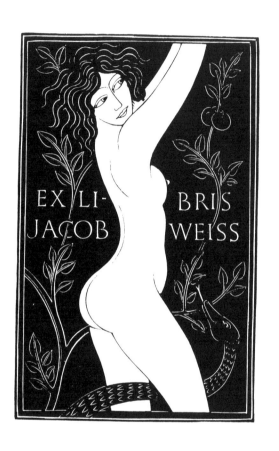

EX LI-
BRIS
JACOB
WEISS

Eric Gill *Plate 10*

EX LIBRIS
VAGN CLEMMENSEN

Gerard Gaudean
Plate 11

EX LIBRIS

GUDRUN CLEMMENSEN

Gerard Gaudean *Plate 12*

EX LIBRIS

G

JØRGEN
VILS-PEDERSEN

Gerard Gaudean *Plate 13*

EX BIBLIOTECA EROTICA GERHARD WUNDERLICH

SHORT STORY
COLLECTION

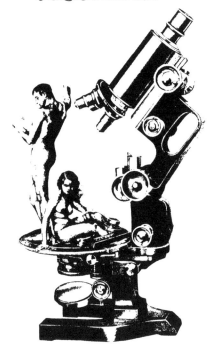

WINWARD PRESCOTT

Franz von Bayros   Plate 15

also a prolific bookplate designer, having nearly three hundred designs to his credit. A large number of these featured nude ladies and sometimes gentlemen. Two examples are shown in *plates 14* and *15*. The first, for Gerhard Wunderlich, is typical of Von Bayros's style. It dates from 1911 and would have caused a certain amount of antagonism. He was in fact prosecuted twice, in 1911 and 1913, for producing offensive drawings. In the first case he was convicted and in the second acquitted.

His own view of the matter is set out clearly in an essay entitled 'Sur ma morale', of which an extract is quoted at the beginning of this book and another follows.

I have always sought out beauty and have attempted to find it in situations which cannot be mentioned in prudish circles – but which prudish hearts cannot do without. I repeat what I shall say on the day of my next trial; I have never served anything but beauty, that divine beauty that I discern in the least of all mortal creation, that I worship in all its personifications, especially in man. And, dear ladies and gentlemen who may chance to read these lines, that man as I see him is that cultured creature who cannot be endangered by gazing at a 'shameless picture' or reading an erotic book. And such a cultured creature cannot in my opinion be shocked by seeing those parts of the anatomy whose very name the dissembling moralists dare not even mention. If these apostles of morality were to be told that their eating habits are far more disgusting than the representation of a loving couple, they would simply fail to understand. Yet I say that a man eating with his knife or mashing up his food on the plate is far more offensive to my susceptibilities than the offence they claim is caused by looking at my pictures.

The second plate, for Winward Prescott, is atypical and, by the style of the microscope, a later example of his work. The triple nosepiece gives the impression that both figures can be seen through the microscope at the same time, this is not technically possible. The attitude of the man, with his back turned, would suggest that reading a book is more interesting than observing a naked lady.

Two of the most prolific Italian bookplate artists of the twentieth century are Italo Zetti (1913–1978) and Franco Brunello. Zetti is represented by two wood engravings each

EXLIBRIS

LVC DE JAEGHER

Italo Zetti *Plate 16*

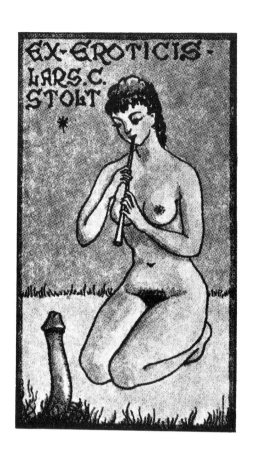

Franco Brunello *Plate 17*

EX·LIBRIS
JØRGEN
VILS *
PEDERSEN

1975
*

Franco Brunello *Plate 18*

JØRGEN
VILS·PEDERSEN

EX LIBRIS

Franco Brunello *Plate 20*

EX EROTICIS

EXLIBRIS EROTICIS

Bodo von Bose   *Plate 22*

•Antonio Samudio   *Plate 23*

depicting three nudes. The frontispiece, a plate for Gorgio Balbi made in 1947, shows a fine figure stripping off in the foreground whilst two others play with a beach ball; the significance of the apples should not go unnoticed. *Plate 16* is for a fellow bookplate artist, the Belgian Luc de Jaegher (b. 1912), who was a contemporary of Severin's and also studied at the Institut Supérieur des Beaux Arts in Antwerp. It shows three nudes playing in a pool observed by Cupid, the initials on his quiver indicating the destinations of his arrows of love.

Plate 17 shows the Brunello design for Lars Stolt, who is the President of the Swedish Bookplate Society and has a large personal collection of erotic and armorial plates. In this one a nude lady is shown charming a well-recognised 'snake'. Three other plates, all with similar theme, are shown for Jorgen Vils-Pedersen. *Plate 18* shows a nubile young lady 'playing with fire'; *plate 19* a black-stockinged nude being assaulted by Cupid with his bow and 'arrow'; and *plate 20* a young couple with a problem. Some may regard this as humorous; others would not see the funny side.

Still on the penile theme, *plate 21* shows another Lars Stolt plate, this time by Eugen Schmidt (b.1910) depicting a young lady riding an orgasmic cockerel. A similar idea is used by Bodo von Bose in his design for I.M. (Joseph Minisalvatje) shown in *plate 22*.

In case it should be thought that attitudes have changed completely since the time that Von Bayros was prosecuted for producing indecent drawings, it should be noted that a bookplate, with an identical design to the previous plates, by Max Lislinger (1895–1983) for Dro Huberman, was one of a number of erotic plates in a major bookplate exhibition in Bogotá, Colombia in 1988. Six of the erotic plates including this one were not illustrated in the official catalogue because the printer refused to print them. Many other erotic plates were printed. It would appear that female nudity, however explicit, was acceptable to that particular printer, but couples shown making love or any form of excited male nudity was not. Needless to say the local Press had a field day at the expense of the printer. Another printer immediately printed the missing plates as a separate

EX LIBRIS BJHJUNOD

M. Ramsbotham *Plate 24*

PER I MIEI LIBRI GALANTI

EX LIBRIS· GINO SABATTINI

Luigi Bompard · *Plate 25*

Ex Libris

ANTONI MARTINEZ

broadsheet, which was distributed throughout the city and also cut up and pasted into the empty spaces in the official catalogue.

An example of an illustration in the exhibition which did not appear to offend the printer is shown in *plate 23*. It is by Antonio Samudio (b.1934) for Benoit Junod, who was the organiser of the exhibition. It shows a young lady holding an open book in her left hand. The significance of the plate lies in the expression of concentration on the face, the position of the legs and what the young lady might be doing with her right hand. Maybe all this was lost on the printer.

Another plate for Benoit Junod is shown in *plate 24*. The design is by Meredith Ramsbotham. It shows a man reading a book in his library surrounded by four nude ladies involved with music, reading, painting and the arts – an ideal design for a bibliophile.

The use of underclothes to provide an erotic effect is seen in the next three plates, all using a display of books as the link to respectability and to validate the raison d'être. The first, *plate 25*, is typical of the late thirties, showing a scantily clad young lady seated on library steps reading a book. It was designed by the Italian artist Luigi Bompard for Gino Sabattini. The same scenario is used in *plate 26* for Antoni Martinez, although in this case the young lady has lost her balance and is left displaying large quantities of stockings, suspender belt, pants and petticoat, to the obvious amazement of the elderly voyeur. *Plate 27* for Karl Astor continues the book theme, showing a bookpile on which is seated a well-endowed young lady in ill-fitting basque, fishnet stockings and gloves, showing a book with indecipherable illustrations to a puzzled Cupid.

An interesting design requiring a considerable degree of artistic licence is shown in *plate 28*. It is by the Viennese artist J.F. Schmid for Franz Adler. A couple locked in an embrace inside a chemical retort, fanned by the flames presumably of passion, appear to produce an instant baby in the adjacent beaker, watched over by the redundant stork. A nice piece of conception and design!

Most bookplate artists at one time or another produce a bookplate for themselves. An example is shown in *plate 29*, where Jacques Rasdolsky, a Belgian artist, has chosen a female nude to

Ex Libris

Karl Astor

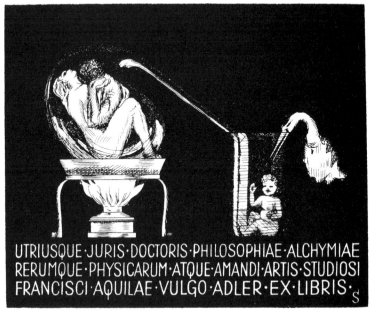

UTRIUSQUE·JURIS·DOCTORIS·PHILOSOPHIAE·ALCHYMIAE
RERUMQUE·PHYSICARUM·ATQUE·AMANDI·ARTIS·STUDIOSI
FRANCISCI·AQUILAE·VULGO·ADLER·EX·LIBRIS·S

J.F. Schmid
Plate 28

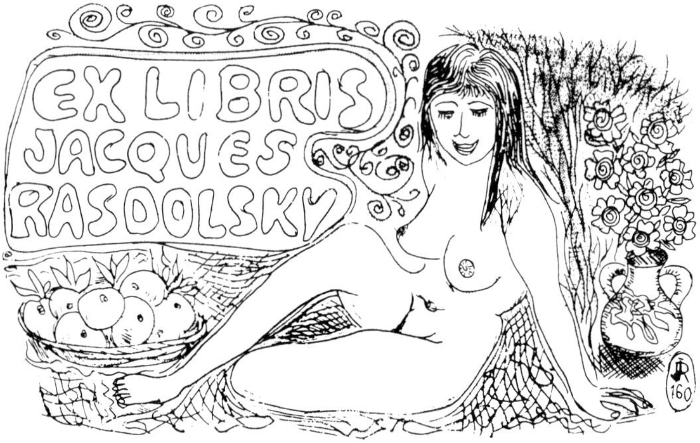
EX LIBRIS
JACQUES
RASDOLSKY
160

J. Rasdolsky *Plate 29*

Francesco Gardeta
Plate 30

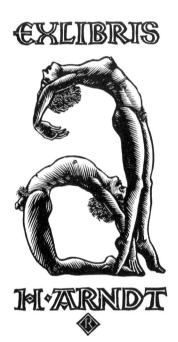

EX LIBRIS J. GARTNER

Paval Hlavaty *Plate 32*

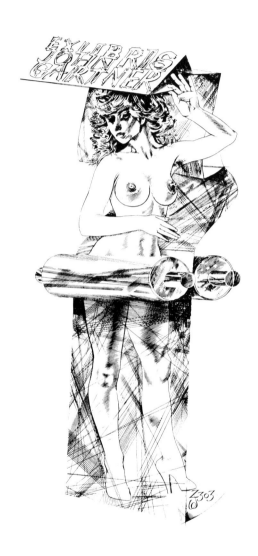

Wim Zwiers *Plate 33*

illustrate his personal plate. The temptation element is present in what appears to be a large basket of apples. Presumably a great deal of temptation is intended.

In *plate 30* a traditional balcony love scene is made more exciting by the fact that 'Juliet' appears to find it necessary to perform the scene in the nude. A strange shadow effect has been used in order to heighten the contrast between body and background. The plate is by the Spanish artist Francesco Gardeta.

A nice little wood engraving by Pam Rueter (b. 1906) shown in *plate 31* makes imaginative use of figure flexibility. It could represent 'a' for acrobat as well as 'a' for Arndt.

The Australian collector John Gartner is well known for his large collection of personal plates, a number of which are erotic in character. Two are shown here. In *plate 32* the Czech artist Paval Hlavaty produces two delightful nude female torsos half hidden in flowers and foliage. The original design is produced in green and is very effective. *Plate 33* is a fine copper engraving by the Dutch artist Wim Zwiers (b.1922, Rotterdam). Zwiers is a prolific artist with many an erotic plate to his name. In this one a nubile young lady is trapped, appropriately enough, between the twin rollers of a printing press.

The final two plates in this volume are to be found in *endpapers 3* and *4* and the back. Ladies bathing is ever a natural excuse for removing clothes. The Estonian artist Richard Kaljo (b.1914, St Petersburg) has a bathing threesome, fully conscious of being observed in *endpaper 3*, which is a wood engraving for Emil Raamat produced in 1965.

The last plate at *endpaper 4* is an amusing and imaginative design for Michala Kuny by the Polish artist Jerzy Drazycki done as a linocut in 1971. It can best be described as an unusual bellpush.

In the space and time available it has only been possible to illustrate a few of the large quantity of erotic bookplates which have been produced for collectors and bibliophiles, and to show a range of artists who have worked and are working in the field. The designs are a product of the artist's imagination and technical ability, combined with the wishes and ideas of the prospective owner who is commissioning the plate. Some owners are entirely happy to leave the whole design to the artist giving him a completely free rein, others wish to have an input to the production to a greater or lesser extent.

The quality, taste and artistic merit of the final result varies enormously. Collectors will have differing opinions as to what is good and what is bad. There is, however, no doubt in my mind that the finest exponent of the erotic bookplate to date is Mark Severin. Sadly we shall have no more plates from the hand of this artist. No matter what the subject or viewpoint it is rare to find an indifferent plate signed with Severin's monogram.

Mark Severin *Plate 34*

BIBLIOGRAPHY

1. Blum, Gernot   *Die Kunst des Erotischen Exlibris*. Berlag Claus Wittal (Wiesbaden, 1986).

2. The Bookplate Society   *Newsletter*, Vols 1–4 (1972–1982)

3. Butler, W.E. and Butler, D.J.   *Modern British Bookplates*. Silent Books (Cambridge, 1990).

4. Butler, W.E., Wilson, J. and Schwab, W.   *The Bookplate Designs of Franz Von Bayros*. James Wilson and the Bookplate Society (1988).

5. Junod, B.   *Ex-Libris O el arte de Identificar sas Libros 1470–1988*. Banco de la Republica, Colombia and Embadja de Suiza.

6. F.I.S.A.E.   *Ex-Libris Artists*. Portugal (1982).

7. Hopt, Andreas and Hopt, Angela   *Erotische Exlibris*. Harenberg Kommunikation (1981).

8. Johnson, F.   *A Treasury of Bookplates*. Dover Publications (New York, 1977).

9. Severin, M. and Reid, A.   *Engraved bookplates 1950–1970*. Private Libraries Association (1972).

10. Skelton, C.   *The Engraved Bookplates of Eric Gill*. Private Libraries Association (1986).

Jerzy Drazycki